ROBERT STEBBI[NGS]
BATS

MAMMAL SOCIETY SERIES

Anthony Nelson

1986 The Mammal Society
First published in 1986 by Anthony Nelson Ltd
PO Box 9, Oswestry, Shropshire SY11 1BY, England.

All rights reserved. No part of this book may be reproduced, stored in a retrieval system, or transmitted in any form or by any means, electronic, mechanical, photocopying or otherwise, without the permission of the publisher.

Series editor Robert Burton
Drawings by Graham Allen (page 4) and
Robert Stebbings (pages 9, 10, 11, 17)
Photographs by Robert Stebbings

Royalties from this series will go to the Mammal Society.

ISBN 0 904614 19 0

Designed by Eric Drewery and Adrian Singer
Printed by K&SC Printers Ltd Tunbridge Wells

Cover: *Barbastelle — a rare species which roosts in vegetation and buildings.*
Inside cover: *The parti-coloured bat, a rare visitor to Britain from eastern Europe*
Title page: *A brown long-eared bat emerging from a tree hole roost.*

The ability to fly separates bats from all other mammals. Worldwide, there are over 950 species of bats in the order Chiroptera which represents nearly one quarter of the mammals. Bats have colonised almost all areas of the world except the polar regions and oceans. They eat many kinds of food from fruit, seeds, nectar and pollen, to blood, fish and other vertebrates, but most species eat insects. All bats in the British Isles and Europe consume insects, with other arthropods such as spiders being taken occasionally.

Thirty one species are currently known to inhabit Europe but only 15 of these are resident in Britain and just seven in Ireland. In recent times the British list of bats has been increased by three because the mouse-eared bat was found to be resident and the grey long eared and Brandt's bats were discovered following their recognition as new species. The parti-coloured bat and Nathusius' pipistrelle are found occasionally as vagrants.

There are two families represented in the British Isles: the Rhinolophidae (the horseshoe bats) and the Vespertilionidae (the vesper bats). Such a small number of bats in our cool temperate climate is hardly surprising because of the difficulties of finding enough insects in bad weather. Indeed, the bats originated in tropical regions and the temperate species have evolved to cope with irregular periods of poor food availability. The physiological mechanisms which allow bats to 'shut down' at any time when food is unobtainable, has enabled them to exploit regions with short summers close to the Arctic circle.

Our bats are able to become torpid at any time, summer or winter, so greatly reducing their energy requirements. In winter, when insects are few, bats hibernate. The alternative to hibernation would be to migrate to a warm climate where they could continue to feed. None of our bats follow this option and some European bats which migrate several hundreds of kilometres do so apparently to find suitable roosting places for hibernation. The tendency to migrate increases the further east one goes across Europe because of the greater severity of winters.

Although they occur almost everywhere, bats have received little attention by naturalists and biologists, and therefore, our knowledge of their natural history is far less than for most other mammals.

Structure and function

Bat wings are relatively little modified from the basic mammalian pattern of forelimb. The forearm consists of a single bone, the radius, with the ulna being reduced to a small slip at the elbow. A clawed thumb projects forward clear of the membrane and is used for grasping and hanging on when the bat lands, as well as for grooming. Bats also often hang by their thumbs, (that is head up) when urinating or defaecating and, by some species when giving birth. The other four fingers all have elongated bones. The metacarpals (palm bones) are greatly lengthened and relatively more so than the phalanges. The third finger extends to the wing tip, and the fifth finger gives rigidity to the wing breadth.

The all-important wing membrane or patagium is tough and elastic with fine musculature, connective tissue and elastic tissue between the skin layers. Bats spend much time grooming the membrane to keep it supple and in good order. The membrane is often torn but the holes usually repair completely. In summer a 10 millimetre hole can disappear in a month or so, but repairing wing tissue more or less stops when the bat is hibernating.

Because of their wings bats have the largest surface area to volume ratio of any mammal. For example, a small species such as the barbastelle, weighing 7 grams and having a volume of 8 cubic centimetres, has a surface area of 220 square centimetres. By contrast, an almost cylindrical mole with the same surface area has a weight and volume ten times greater.

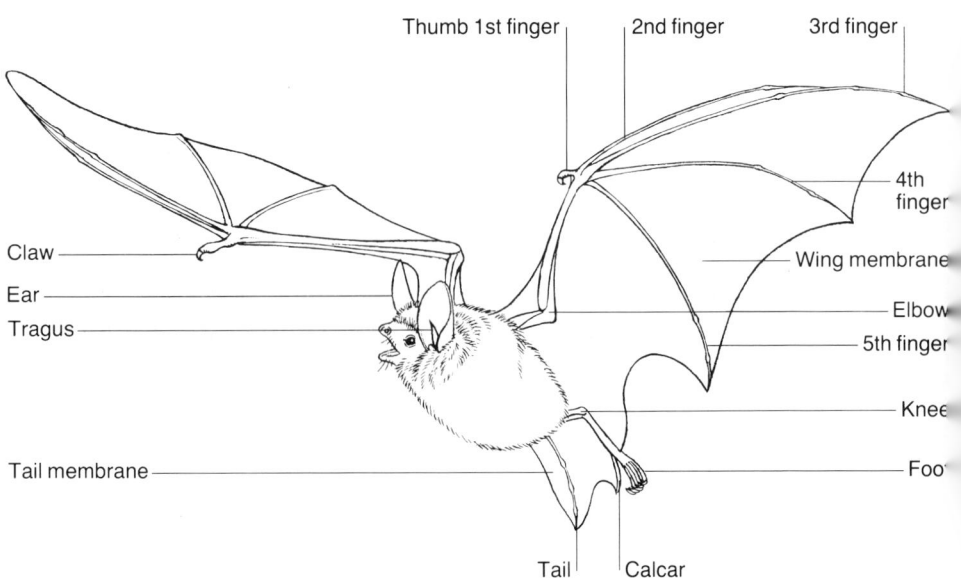

A further membrane encloses the tail. It is stiffened at the edge by the calcar, which is attached to the ankle and extends from one third to threequarters towards the tail, depending on the species. In some species the calcar may be partially bony but in others it is cartilaginous. The knee bends in the opposite direction to that of other mammals, so that the legs, feet and tail may be lowered in flight to act as flaps and thereby increase manoeuvrability. The tail membrane is sometimes used as a scoop for catching food, or to create a bag in which large prey may be tucked or manipulated in flight.

Natterer's bats have a row of sensory bristles along the edge of the tail membrane. This species uses its tail to flick a perched moth into the air before catching it, so the bristles presumably tell the bat when the insect is touched. The females of some species drop their baby at birth into the membrane, before encouraging it to attach itself to the mothers' nipple.

There are some structural and functional differences between members of the two bat families in Britain. The hindfoot in all species has five toes of more or less equal size with highly curved and sharp claws. The feet allow bats to hang upside down in a relaxed position so that they may continue hanging even when dead. However, the horseshoe bats have weak hindlimbs and bodies which are approximately circular in cross section, in contrast with the vesper bats which have relatively robust hindlimbs and dorso-ventrally flattened bodies. As a consequence, vesper bats can crawl and some species, like pipistrelles, can even run quadrupedally, whereas the horseshoe bats cannot hold their body off a horizontal surface. They progress on the ground by leaping and flapping clumsily or by dragging themselves backwards. This also means that horseshoe bats tend to roost in places where they can fly direct to the roost and, with a quick twist, throw their feet up and clutch the roof to achieve a hanging position immediately. Vesper bats, on the other hand, frequently live in crevies which require them to land and crawl to the roost, where they may turn around to hang. Often vesper bats crawl into horizontal crevices and, in hibernation, some may be found with their heads uppermost.

When hanging, horseshoe bats have their heads at right angles (or even a greater angle) to their spines, while vesper bats hold their heads in line, nose downwards. Torpid horseshoe bats wrap their wings around them so that often only the tips of the ears are showing but vesper bats hold their wings to their sides with the head and body exposed. The long-eared bats are the exception. They tend to roost in very cold places and, when hanging 'free', may partly fold their wings around themselves and bring the tail membrane forward to cover the belly.

The heads of bats often appear strange because of the large ears and various growths around the nostrils. These are associated with the broadcasting of sound and receipt of the returning echoes. The vesper bats mostly have simple doglike noses. Sounds for echolocation are emitted through the open mouth and echoes are picked up by ears whose size depends on the way the species searches for its prey. Fast flying, loudly shouting noctules have short, relatively streamlined ears, whereas the much quieter Bechstein's bats, have large ears and fly slowly feeding around trees and among foliage.

Most extreme in terms of ear size are the long-eared bats (and to a lesser extent the barbastelle) which emit whispering sounds through their nostrils with closed mouths. They fly slowly as they feed in and around foliage, even hovering to pluck insects off leaves and twigs.

Horseshoe bats also emit echolocation pulses through their nostrils but they have elaborate skin growths, including the 'horseshoe' shape, around the nostrils. The sounds are modified and directed by the noseleaves, and close observation of the 'horseshoe' during sound emission shows that it is like a variable-geometry, parabolic radar dish. It changes shape so that it is sometimes dished to produce a narrow beam of sound, while at other times it is flattened to spread sound widely.

Daubenton's bat echolocating just at point of take-off.

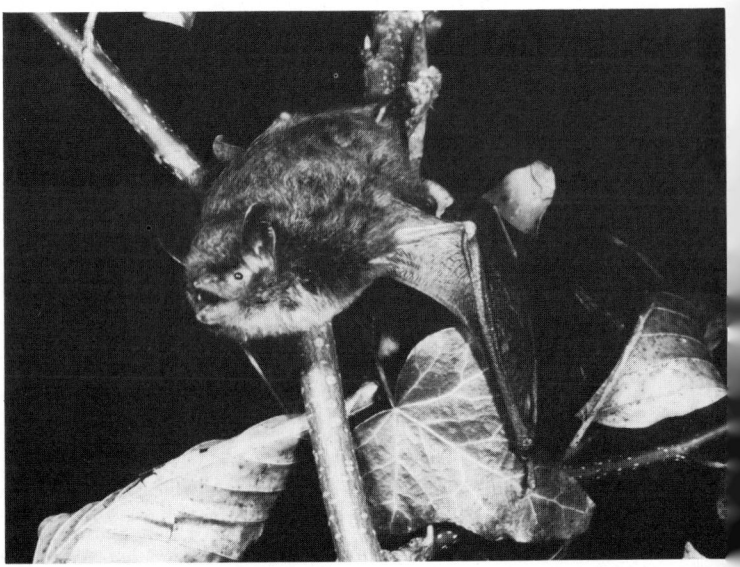

Colony — a definition

Daubenton's nursery with nearly full grown juveniles recognisable by their grey fur.

The concept of a colony of bats is important to understand.

A colony of bats is a group of animals of one species in an area, which normally relate to each other exclusively.

At various times of the year members of the colony will meet up with other members, and sometimes a substantial number (perhaps over half) may occupy a roost simultaneously.

The term 'population' may include bats of one species but including members of several colonies: or it can mean bats of all species living in an area. Often caves contain bats from several colonies.

Flight and Feeding

In flight, bats constantly alter the wing shape in response to changing needs, particularly by increasing camber (the curve of the wing) to prevent stalling at slower speeds just before landing. Bat species have differingly shaped wings to cope with the way they utilise their habitat and how they search for and catch food. With much practice, some bats may be identified in flight by the shape of the wings, flight patterns and type of habitat in which they feed.

Of Britain's 15 species, some, like noctules and the closely related Leisler's bats, have long, narrow, pointed wings and they pursue prey mostly in the air, well clear of vegetation. They fly fast over long distances, and are able to make rapid but sweeping turns. They are clumsy on the ground but, nevertheless like most bats, may catch some prey on the ground and they can take off from flat surfaces.

By contrast, long-eared bats and horseshoe bats have broad, rounded-tipped wings which are used for highly manoeuvrable flight, twisting and turning among vegetation. Long-eared bats frequently hover when searching for prey and immediately before alighting.

Fast flying noctules have streamlined wings with the forearm bone (radius) being flattened, especially on the dorsal surface to which the membrane is attached, while in the long-eared bats, for instance, the bone is circular with membranes attached at about

Brandt's bat eating a moth.

A brown long-eared bat in flight. Note the closed mouth as this bat echolocates through its nostrils, like horseshoe bats.

mid-point. Not only does the noctule's bone structure result in less drag, but a more streamlined profile is created by bands of hair in front and behind the forearm on the under surface. The hair helps to reduce eddies and facilitates a smooth airflow over both surfaces.

Because of the difficulty we have in observing bats in the dark, we do not know where most feed or what they feed on. It is known, however, that each species has its preferred feeding habitat which varies seasonally according to the availability of insects. For example, Daubenton's bat (also known as the water bat) frequents open, slow-flowing water, where it flies a few centimetres above the surface catching emergent insects. After a storm, when the river is in spate and there are no insects, it moves to grassland on the lee side of woodland.

Greater horseshoe bats tend to prefer the seclusion of woodland in which to feed, especially at dusk, but they will also feed in open pasture. Their choice of habitat depends on the behaviour of the insects. In spring, even after a warm sunny day,

Outlines and sections through the wing and forearm of the Noctule (upper) and a brown long-eared bat (lower).

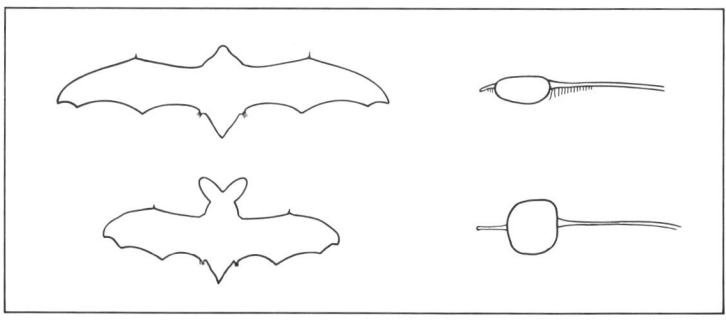

the evenings may be cold. Insects which emerge from pasture fly into warmer shelter belts or woodland, and that is where the bats feed. However, if, after a hot day, the night remains warm with many insects emerging, especially cockchafers, then greater horseshoes will feed over pasture. At this time they behave like flycatchers. Flying out over grassland, they catch beetles and carry them to a perch in a tree, bush or wall. A cockchafer weighing one gram is eaten in about four minutes. The head, legs, wings and wing cases fall to the ground and accumulate to reveal the whereabouts of bat perches.

Having finished one insect, the bat takes off to catch another. It seems the buzzing of the beetles, as they warm up to take off, may be heard by bats who, initially, home in by listening before relying on their sophisticated sonar for the catch.

Later in the year greater horseshoe bats specialise in feeding low over pasture, flying in and out of grass tussocks to pick up noctuid moths and small dung beetles such as *Aphodes*. In autumn the large annual dor beetles form a major part of the diet just prior to hibernation. Like cockchafers, these beetles are likely to be picked off the ground or just at take-off, because they fly too fast for horseshoes to catch. Greater horseshoe bats have been seen landing on the ground to take dung flies and other emergent insects from cow pats, and this behaviour has been

Feeding zones of different species.

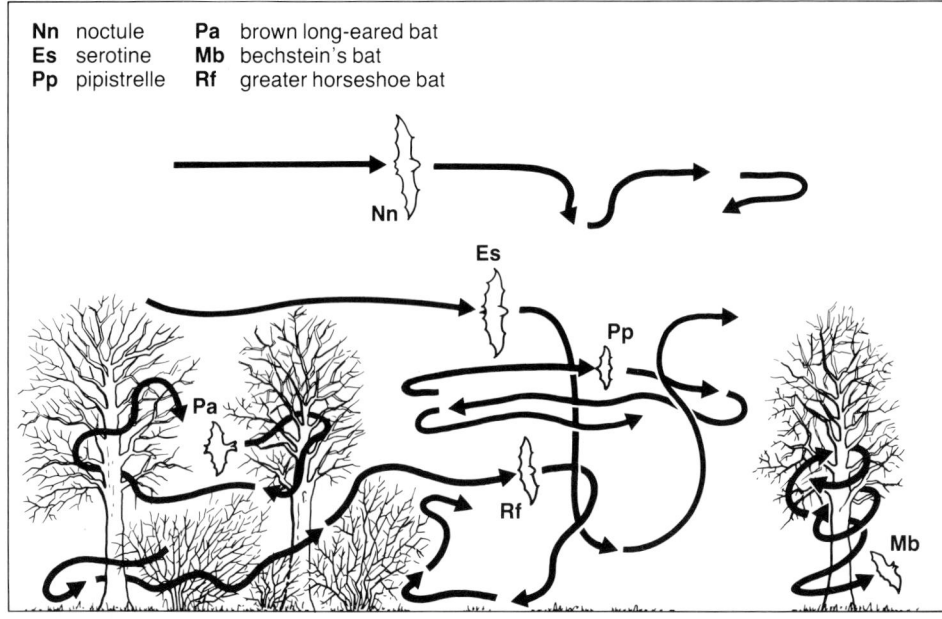

Nn	noctule	**Pa**	brown long-eared bat
Es	serotine	**Mb**	bechstein's bat
Pp	pipistrelle	**Rf**	greater horseshoe bat

discovered in several bat species by pieces of vegetation turning up in their droppings.

Serotines, which have large, broad wings similar to the greater horseshoe bat's, specialise in feeding over pasture, along high hedges or on the edge of woodland. Being one of Britain's big bags, they prefer large insects, but rather than behaving like a flycatcher, serotines prefer to eat their food while in flight. Having caught a large beetle, a serotine will cruise around slowly, chewing and dropping the wingcases and legs. Wingcases found on the ground often show the characteristic 1 millimetre diameter punctures made by the serotine's large canine teeth.

Pipistrelles also feed in a variety of habitats. Typically they chase about in the open over gardens or pasture, but they are

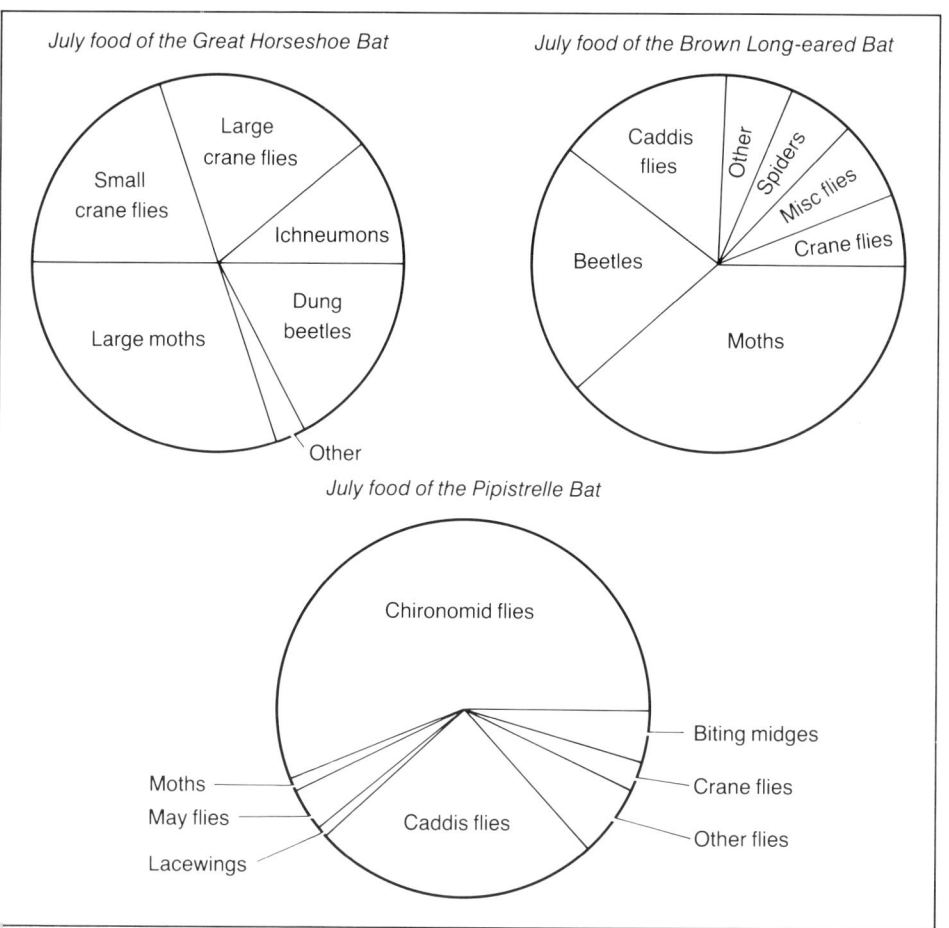

frequently seen low over water catching emergent caddis, mayflies or blackflies. They are readily distinguished from Daubenton's bat because they appear rather untidy and hurried, often leaping well above the water while Daubenton's bats are usually sedate, with a deceptively slow, vibrating, level flight about 10 centimetres above the surface. On wet windy nights pipistrelles may be seen feeding in woodland, but they tend to prefer mature, relatively open stands. The similarly shaped and sized whiskered bat is more often found in woodland, as it is much more adept at dodging around foliage in pursuit of small insects like micro-moths and flies.

A staple diet for most bats is crane flies, because of the wide range of different species and differing sizes which are available in every month of the year. Also, crane flies tend to fly slowly and hence may be readily caught.

Why feed at night?

Bats were subjected to a number of selective pressures over the course of their evolution. Insects represent an energy rich diet, but when is it best to catch them? Nothing is known of the early evolution of bats before the mid-Eocene (55 million years ago), when bats similar to present forms were flying. However, birds, which evolved from reptilian stock, were probably in the air and eating flying insects when the ancestors of bats were first leaping off trees. No doubt some birds would be predatory, quite prepared to catch anything flying in the open such as bats. However, if you are going to feed on insects the best time to eat would be when the highest densities are available. The greatest number of insects fly in the two hours after sunset, when they are still warm from the day and air humidities are high. (Many insects hide in damp places by day to prevent dessication.) There is then a gradual decline in numbers of airborn insects through the night, and a slight peak again just before dawn. More insects fly when it is warm and humid, but few fly when it is cold, or in wind speeds above 10 knots, but both insects and bats often fly in the rain, even in thunderstorms. The problem with exploiting this nocturnal food is that specialised senses are required to locate it. Birds, like the swallows, developed acute vision to cope with target-discrimination and range-finding in their high speed chasing of diurnal insects. The eyesight of some bats may be sufficiently good to see some insects at dusk, but they have opted for feeding in darkness. This required the development of echolocation as their major sense for food detection and capture.

Feeding times

Any animal with a high metabolic rate and a food which is very patchy in space and time, needs to know when to feed, and more important, when to give up and go home. If a bat is already thin, it would spell disaster if it woke up, flew out and spent energy searching for food, only to fail. If a bat is to arouse from its day time torpor, it is best therefore to choose a warm night with adequate insects.

It seems likely that bats are constantly assessing the balance between food intake and energy expenditure and so opt to return to roost and torpor if their energy gain falls too much.

Different bat species emerge at different times but their average emergence time is related to sunset. Noctules tend to emerge first, shortly after sunset, with the first pipistrelles about 20 minutes later. At the other extreme, brown long-eared and Daubenton's bats can be very late emergers, often coming out when it is completely dark. However, these are only generalisations and there is a wider variation not just between species but between colonies of the same species. Also, emergence on successive nights is highly variable. Windy, cold and wet nights seem to delay emergence, while cloud on warm nights tends to encourage an early exit. However, there may be all sorts of factors involved, including how hungry the bats are, whether there are young to feed, and even perhaps, the bats' ability to

Cockchafer beetles are among the most important food for large bats in spring.

predict the best time to go foraging. Much more research is needed to answer these questions.

Feeding behaviour patterns and flight durations are very variable and we know little about most species. Pipistrelles take a long time to fill their stomachs because they generally eat small insects living in dense swarms. This means that they have to eat many hundreds, which even at a peak of one insect caught every 5 seconds, still takes perhaps two hours.

A greater horseshoe bat, on the other hand, feeding on one cockchafer every four minutes, catches a stomach-full in less than half an hour. Having emerged, bats feed for varying lengths of time. With sparse prey they often return within minutes and do not emerge again. Plentiful food results in hours spent away from the day roost. For the best studied species, such as the pipistrelle and greater horseshoe bat, we know there may be a single flight at dusk on some nights with bats returning within an hour, or as many as ten separate flights of differing durations and not always returning to the day roosts between them. Several species are known to use regular temporary roosts at night, termed feeding perches. Best known perches are those in porches or under low, wide eaves, or in outbuildings as used by long-eared bats. These sites are recognised by the accumulation of moth wings, but usually the absence of bat droppings.

Metabolism

One of the characteristics of mammals is that they are endotherms. This means that they generate heat in their bodies. The heat is used to regulate their body temperature within fine limits, an ability called homoiothermy. However, bats in England have been termed heterothems because they do not generally maintain a constant temperature and can become almost 'cold blooded', by letting their temperature drop. Animals like man normally have a temperature range of about one degree through the day, while bats, even in summer, may have temperatures ranging from 15° Celsius during torpor to 40° Celsius while flying.

Why should bats have evolved such an extreme metabolism? Maintenance of high body temperatures rapidly uses up energy, which needs to be replaced by frequent meals. We have already seen that although insect food is high in energy, its availability to bats is extremely variable and unpredictable. One night may have a hundred times more insects flying than the next. Such a patchy food source can only be utilised efficiently by animals which are able to significantly reduce their energy consumption when food is absent. Bats do this by becoming torpid and lowering their body temperatures to approximately air temperature at almost any time.

During the day bats are often resting and torpid. With the approach of dusk, body temperatures may rise to 40° Celsius (or slightly more), with heart beat rates jumping from 200–300 to about 1000 per minute at take off. On returning from feeding, body temperatures remain at 32° – 35° Celsius for digestion. Then after an hour or two, the bats drop their temperature to that of the surrounding air. This is achieved quickly by the bats slowly waving their wings, which act as efficient radiators.

Pregnant females have some different needs. If breeding is to be successful, births must coincide with peak availability of insects, (which in Britain is usually at the end of June). This is because lactation is the most energy costly phase in a bat's life. In early pregnancy females are heterothermic. They readily become torpid when digestion is complete or when food is unavailable. By mid pregnancy, many become homoiothermic and maintain a high body temperature throughout the 24 hours to aid rapid development of the foetus. This is only possible for those bats with adequate body food reserves, but bats have three ploys they can adopt to improve their energy efficiency.

First they choose roosts in warm places: at the top of domes, in the entrances of caves or in house roofs heated by the sun. Secondly, they form tight clusters with other bats, so that each individual expends minimal energy in keeping warm (usually about 30° Celsius is preferred), and thirdly, they try to eat more. Late in pregnancy, when the foetus occupies much of the abdomen, some bats become heterothermic again because they cannot eat much.

After birth and throughout suckling, bats are normally homoiothermic. If food is unavailable, through prolonged bad weather, the mother's milk dries up and she usually deserts her baby, which dies a few days later. Sometimes whole colonies have to abandon their young.

Greater horseshoe bats — 167 in hibernation.

Hibernation

Towards the end of September females and immature bats begin to increase their weight quickly if food is plentiful. Being heterothermic at this time saves energy and therefore helps in gaining weight. Adult males tend to be homiothermic and remain thin as they spend much of their time attracting females and mating, but little in feeding.

Before hibernation body weight increases by about one third and bats move into their hibernation sites. Initiation of hibernation is not a sudden event but is a gradual change involving variations in the physiology. Bats also change from waking and feeding nightly to remaining torpid for longer periods. Even in mid-winter all bats wake at intervals, with those roosting in the warmest sites (such as horseshoe bats) waking most frequently. When awake, the bats may fly and attempt to feed, or they may groom, before returning to torpor.

Why should bats awaken in winter? The main purpose is to readjust the various chemical balances within the body. Most food reserves are fat and, as this is metabolised, excess water as well as other, often toxic, wastes are produced in the tissues. One of the actions immediately upon waking is to urinate. Indeed it has been speculated that initiation of arousal may be stimulated by a full bladder!

There is no very clear distinction between cave roosting species and the others. Noctules, Leisler's bats, pipistrelles and serotines virtually never enter caves, but all others use them to a greater or less extent. All species are found in buildings, and all except the horseshoe bats roost in trees. (One lesser horseshoe bat colony was found in a large hollow cedar in Somerset.) Whatever the

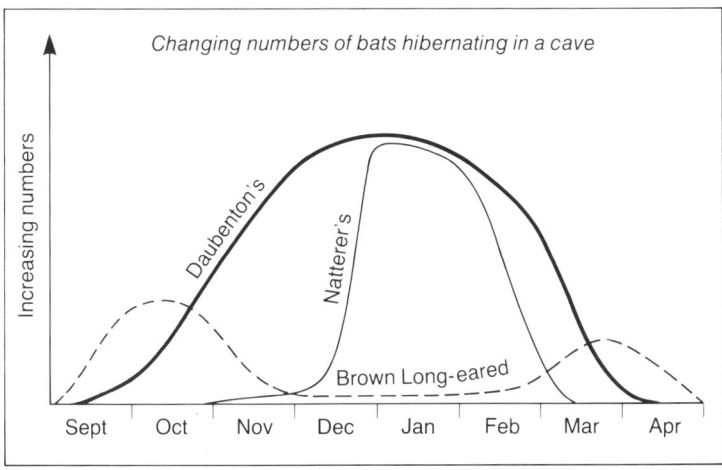

chosen site for hibernation, it must provide seclusion and safety from predators, and protection from extreme temperature fluctuations. It must also be humid.

Cave-dwelling bats choose sites which have little temperature variation. Each species has its preferred range of temperatures, with greater horseshoe bats preferring the warmest parts while brown long-eared bats and barbastelles like the coldest areas. Also, within each species, there are patterns of choice which are dependent on age, sex, weight of bat and time of winter. Generally warm temperatures are selected at first, and cool ones towards the end of hibernation. Old heavy females select warmer places than young lightweight males. A ten year old, 30 gram female greater horseshoe bat, may be found at 11° Celsius in November, but in March, weighing 22 grams, it will be roosting at 8° Celsius.

Brown long-eared bats often visit caves in early autumn, when caves at about 10° Celsius are the coldest roost sites available, but move out again in December when colder temperatures prevail in other roosts, for example tree holes. Barbastelles are most extreme, apparently preferring conditions around freezing point. These rare bats visit cave entrances in very low temperatures, usually only when it has been below −10° Celsius for some days.

Apart from the long-eared and the horseshoe bats, Daubenton's bats are the earliest to enter caves, often in September. The older adult females are the first to enter, usually very fat and weighing up to 12 grams, followed by adult males and then the relatively thin juveniles of the year which weigh about 8.5 grams. Their numbers gradually increase until a peak is reached, usually in early January. Natterer's bats by contrast tend to move in to caves suddenly in December, reaching a peak in January and then leaving gradually in the following two months.

Social organisation and roost behaviour

We know little of the interactions of bats in colonies or of competition between species. Brown long-eared bat colonies appear to have all sexes and age groups freely intermixing and forming clusters at all seasons. Several adult males may roost together with females, even in the mating period. The rare but closely related grey long-eared bat, by contrast, normally has females roosting separately from males, with only one adult male found in close association with the females. As the sexes are born in equal numbers the implication is that one male is dominant and excludes all others. It is noticeable that the incumbent male is always a large specimen.

For most species, adult females, with some immature females and males, form clusters in preparation for the birth of young in June or July. The pregnant females will have started to gather in small groups in spring at sites often termed transition roosts. Gradually groups join up, as they move to other roosts. When food is sparse, small groups may serve to avoid competition for food while the bats are heterothermic. Later in pregnancy when food is more plentiful the bats become homoiothermic and need to cluster in large groups for the energetic advantages.

Adult males keep in touch by briefly visiting the nurseries and other roosts where members of the colonies are to be found. Adult males remain semi-torpid much of the summer, sometimes sharing roosts with other adult males or more frequently, with immatures. Only just prior to the mating season does a dominant male occupy a roost exclusively, and it is assumed that other males have been driven off. It is not known whether bats defend feeding areas, but they have been observed apparently chasing others away aggressively and then returning to a previously occupied beat to continue feeding.

Roosts are sometimes occupied by two or more species and mostly these associations appear friendly. Summer roosts in trees and buildings have colonies of various combinations, with bats

Fifty five juvenile brown long-eared bats forming part of a 200 strong colony in a roof.

sometimes touching. Brown long-eared bats are often found with others especially Daubenton's, Natterer's, whiskered or Brandt's bats. Buildings frequently shelter several species but the various bats may not come into contact. Pipistrelles are particularly irritable and are usually found roosting apart from other species.

In winter as in summer, bats tend to be secretive and few can be found. Therefore our view of what is normal behaviour in bats is based on relatively small samples of accessible animals. In caves and tunnels most bats are solitary or occasionally form small groups. Mixed species groups are found sometimes with the *Myotis* bats, including Daubenton's, Natterer's, whiskered, Brandt's and mouse-eared bats being found in various combinations. Other species maybe nearby but not actually touching.

A mating group of pipistrelles in a tree hole.

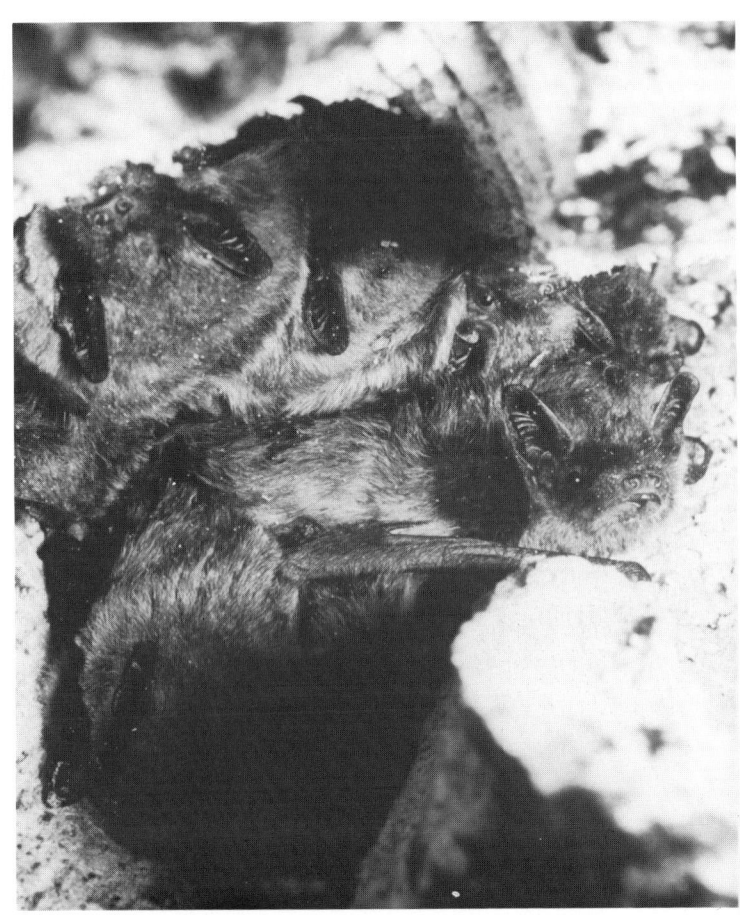

Breeding

The principal mating period is in the autumn, beginning in September, and gradually falling off into hibernation. Like many other bat species, especially in temperate regions, British bats have a feature in their reproduction which is unique among mammals. Males may store mature sperm for many months before mating and females store it after mating, although there are variations between species as to which sex stores sperm longest. For example, noctules and pipistrelles are generally mated before hibernation, whereas the incidence of mated female Daubenton's bats increases steadily throughout the winter. The significance of this is unknown.

The social organisation of mate selection is little known, but it appears that in most species, solitary adult males occupy traditional roosts in the autumn, the whereabouts of which are probably known to many females of a colony. All adult males undergo spermatogenesis in the summer when they may be found solitary or roosting with other males, both adult and immature. By September one male remains, others having gone, presumably driven off by this dominant one.

A pipistrelle nursery colony. Note the baby being nursed.

Male noctules and Leisler's bats emerge from their holes after dark and fly around slowly, calling loudly every second or so, using high intensity sounds clearly audible to us rather than the ultrasonic cries which they normally use for prey location and obstacle avoidance. They keep within about 300 metres of their roost, returning to it after a few minutes. There they wait, and if no females arrive, they fly around calling again. Females eventually go to the males, and one noctule has been recorded as having up to 18 females in his hole. Mating is accompanied by much noise, usually with the male screeching and eventually mounting the female from the back, holding her neck in his mouth and curling his tail beneath her. The large penis (which is always obvious in bats) has a small bone (*os penis or baculum*) in the tip (glans), which in some species is large enough to give some additional support to the erect penis. (The shape and size of the *os penis* is characteristic for each species.) Coition may last for half an hour and upon separation both partners usually wash and groom vigorously.

Although eggs develop in the ovary in the summer prior to copulation, ovulation does not occur until the following spring, and fertilisation depends on stored sperm.

After insemination, sperm becomes lined up against the wall of the uterus and it is released again at ovulation. It is not clear, precisely, what controls the date of ovulation but higher roost temperatures, especially in the second half of hibernation, result in an earlier ovulation.

The fertilized egg implants on the uterine wall, (usually the right horn in bats), and development proceeds. The rate of development is dependent upon roost temperature and the weather conditions, which control the availability of insects. In cold, wet, windy weather, pregnant bats become torpid and foetal growth slows or stops. Cold weather close to birth can result in abortion of young or abandonment of the babies, especially if the mothers cannot catch sufficient food. A single young is born after mid-June or in early July but, exceptionally, births may occur from the beginning of June to mid-August. Twins are known in several species, especially amongst pipistrelles in Scotland.

The mothers usually separate slightly from the main colony when about to give birth but they return to the cluster a few hours later. The young are born blind but their eyes open within five days, at which time ears become erect. Although they appear more or less naked, short hair is already growing, in six days the back is covered and at about ten days old the belly fur hides the pink skin. At birth, heads are large, but so too are the sharply

Wing of a 20-day Daubenton's bat showing translucent cartilaginous joints and the parasitic mites that are common on juveniles.

clawed feet which are nearly adult size and vital for hanging onto the mother. The baby usually attaches itself to one of the two pectorally placed nipples and immediately begins to suck.

It often used to be stated that bats carry their young for the first two or three weeks of life when out foraging. This is now known to be untrue. In fact, it would be very difficult for the mother to carry even a newborn baby, which may weigh one third of her weight, and still manoeuvre efficiently to catch insects. However, babies, even more or less fully grown ones, are sometimes carried from one roost to another if conditions in the first become unsuitable. Occasionally, young born shortly after dusk will be carried, but it is not certain whether this may be a response to disturbance by observers.

The movement of bats into nursery roots occurs at different times for various species. These nurseries usually contain the pregnant females of one colony, with a few immatures of both sexes. Generally all nurseries are established by mid-June, but movement between roosts still occurs if the conditions are not suitable. We do not know precisely why a colony moves, but presumably temperatures in the roost are unsuitable or food sources may be too distant.

Young bats are suckled at intervals during the night when mothers return from feeding. They remain attached to the mother

for much of the day for the first ten days or so. Wing stretching begins at a very early age and in some species first flying attempts are made in roosts at about 17 to 18 days. Outside flights take place after three weeks when wing bones are almost full size. Ossification of bones is virtually complete within two months.

Suckling ceases after 30 to 40 days and the mothers then leave the nursery. However, they appear to remain in contact with the juveniles but do not necessarily roost in the same site. Mother bats apparently show their young alternative roosts but nothing is known about how the young learn to find and catch insects.

Most species mature in their first year and many females produce young at 12 months old. Greater horseshoe bats are exceptional, with most females giving birth for the first time at four years. A few are much older and some females do not breed every year, especially when young. Greater horseshoe males generally mature in their second year while males of other species mature in their first.

Populations

Historically, bats were essentially forest dwelling animals, roosting in tree holes and exploiting insects caught over or within the canopy, in clearings or along woodland edges, including rivers and edges of lakes. With changes in habitat and climate, one would expect changes in relative abundance, species composition and distribution of populations. This is shown by changes in the distribution of the Bechstein's bat. Evidence from archaeological deposits at Grimes Graves, Norfolk, suggests that it was very common 3500 years ago in East Anglia, where large areas were under permanent deciduous forest. Nowadays the species is not only unknown in eastern England but it is extremely rare even where it does occur in the southern counties. Although a rare bat throughout its range, reasonable numbers are found in well forested regions of central Europe which shows its preference for high forest.

As Britain's forests were felled from Neolithic times onward to make clearances for agriculture and later to provide charcoal for iron smelting, so the high forest dependent species would have declined, and those species prospered which were better able to exploit open range habitats. Loss of forest reduced roost sites and altered insect species composition (and possibly abundance), but the next big change was the building of churches and houses which bats quickly adopted as roosts.

Pipistrelles, which would have lived in cool hollow trees, have,

Nathusius' pipistrelle, a recent vagrant.

perhaps, benefitted most from buildings, especially the south sides where their weather coverings heat up quickly in the sun. Colonies of 2000 pipistrelles were probably fairly common at one time, but recent observations suggest there have been large and rapid declines of this, our most common species. In six years from 1978 to 1984 average colony size fell from 119 bats to 55. The main cause appeared to be bad weather at critical times, especially in late June when lack of food causes mothers to abandon their babies. Because females on average produce less than one young per year, recovery of populations after such a decline will be slow.

Greater horseshoe bats which used to be distributed south of the Thames to mid-Wales in the late 19th century, are now extinct over half their former range. Large colonies of the species in some of the cathedrals such as Canterbury, Winchester and Wells, were killed or removed, and many others in caves and buildings were deliberately killed or accidently destroyed through woodworm treatment or fire.

Formerly greater horseshoe bats used to have their nurseries mainly in south facing caves where they chose warm high domes close to the entrance. Unfortunately, there were no documented counts of the huge clusters of horseshoe bats which used to occur. However, the size of guano piles can be measured and there are some people who have seen large groups of greater horseshoes in the last 25 years. Aggregations of bats in several roosts in west Wales and Cornwall covered areas up to 10 square metres. In such large colonies, the bats pack in at 1000 to 1500 bats per square metre and even higher densities may be found when bats hang onto each other. Most of these colonies have vanished and there are now only eight major colonies left in Britain. The largest totals no more than 600 animals when the young fly in August, a figure which is tiny compared with the size of past colonies. Bats are particularly vulnerable to catastrophies because of their gregarious habit. Many sudden declines can be attributed to the destruction of nursery colonies which usually contain most of the breeding potential for a large area. For instance, in west Wales the greater horseshoe bat colony occupies an area of about 2000 square kilometres, so, by eliminating one colony, a huge area could become devoid of that species. Members of the colony, roost in a large number of sites in the year. The 500 bats in this area may have as many as 300 different places they use for shelter, though some may be occupied for only one day.

Chances for survival from one year to the next are very variable for any aged bat, but juveniles are most at risk from adverse factors. Bad weather in the autumn of birth can prevent the accumulation of food reserves prior to hibernation and first year mortality can be severe, with only 10 to 20 per cent of young surviving. Conversely, a good autumn may result in almost all juvenile bats surviving their first year. Second year animals stand a much better chance of surviving and the survival rate appears to improve with age. This is not only to be expected but is vital for bats as they breed so slowly.

Average lifespan for most species is 4–5 years but it is about 6·5 years for greater horseshoe bats. A few bats survive 30 years (but their teeth are very worn by then).

Although equal numbers of each sex are born it appears males' survival is less than females. For many years the converse was thought to be true but this knowledge was based on observations of hibernating populations in which males predominated by up to 60 per cent. It is now known that males require slightly different conditions from females, hence the discrepancy. Females are apparently missing from known sites and are not caught.

Where do bats live?

Bats may be found virtually anywhere. While most seek seclusion and relatively dark places, others may be found in exposed sites, in crevices on trees or walls of houses, near the eaves, behind drainpipes or an endless number of other places. After a lifetime of studying bats I am no longer surprised by where they are found. Some roost underground in scree slopes and in France they are said to live in badger setts. It is likely that bats will be found anywhere if searched for sufficiently.

Few bats now have nursery sites in cold places such as caves and mines, but at least eight species may be found roosting in such places. Tunnels of all kinds, ice houses, cellars, hollow walls, sewers, bridges, fortifications both derelict and restored, and any kind of underground places are used for hibernation. The other species hibernate in buildings and hollow trees, which also constitute the most important summer roosts, although some nurseries occur in caves, mines and tunnels (for example canal tunnels).

A grille protects hibernating bats from disturbance.

Bat boxes provide artificial tree holes for bat colonies.

Conservation

Surveying caves for hibernating bats. This one is 40 metres deep.

Because bats have declined in many areas, and for reasons due to man's activities, all British bats were protected in 1981, under the Wildlife and Countryside Act. It is now an offence to disturb or handle bats, or to sell, exchange or barter them without first having a licence from the Nature Conservancy Council (NCC). It is also illegal to damage a bat roost, including those in houses, without first informing the NCC of the intent and seeking advice on how to avoid harming the bats. This is important because exclusion or killing of colonies in buildings is likely to have contributed substantially to the demise of bats.

Timber treatments with highly toxic chemicals to kill woodworm and fungus infestations in buildings, have undoubtedly killed many colonies of bats. The main culprits were the insecticides Lindane and Dieldrin and the fungicide pentachlorophenol. All three chemicals are highly persistent and easily absorbed by the bats, which may return to a death trap many months after a treatment. Relatively non-toxic chemicals such as the artificial pyrethroids (eg Permethrin) are now available and these are increasingly being used in all buildings because they are much safer for humans, too.

The pipistrelle — our smallest and most abundant bat.

Resident and vagrant bats in Britain

Species	Distribution	Wing span	Weight
		millimetres	grams
1 GREATER HORSESHOE BAT (Rhinolophus ferrumequinum)	South Wales and south-west England	340 – 390	13 – 34
2 LESSER HORSESHOE BAT (Rhinolophus hipposideros)	West England and Wales north to Yorkshire	225 – 250	4 – 9
3 WHISKERED BAT (Myotis mystacinus)	Probably north to Scottish border	210 – 240	4 – 9
4 BRANDT'S BAT (Myotis brandtii)	Probably north to Scottish border	210 – 255	5 – 10
5 DAUBENTON'S BAT (Myotis daubentonii)	Throughout Britain	230 – 270	6 – 12
6 NATTERER'S BAT (Myotis nattereri)	Britain except possibly north-west Scotland	250 – 300	7 – 12
7 BECHSTEIN'S BAT (Myotis bechsteinii)	Central — southern England	250 – 300	7 – 13
8 MOUSE-EARED BAT (Myotis myotis)	Confined to south coast	365 – 450	25 – 45
9 PIPISTRELLE (Pipistrellus pipistrellus)	Throughout Britain	190 – 250	3 – 9
10 SEROTINE (Eptesicus serotinus)	South of a line from Aberystwyth to the Wash	340 – 380	15 – 35
11 LEISLER'S BAT (Nyctalus leisleri)	Britain north to Scottish border	280 – 340	11 – 20
12 NOCTULE (Nyctalus noctula)	Britain north to Scottish border	320 – 390	15 – 40
13 BARBASTELLE (Barbastella barbastellus)	Britain north to Scottish border	245 – 280	6 – 13
14 BROWN LONG-EARED BAT (Plecotus auritus)	Throughout Britain	230 – 285	6 – 12
15 GREY LONG-EARED BAT (Plecotus austriacus)	Confined to south coast counties	255 – 300	7 – 14
Vagrants			
NATHUSIUS' PIPISTRELLE (Pipistrellus nathusii)	Three found in south and east England	220 – 270	4 – 10
PARTI-COLOURED BAT (Vespertilio murinus)	Several found in England and Scotland	260 – 330	11 – 16

31

For identification of bats from specimens or their signs see:

Stebbings R. E. (1986) *Which bat is it? A guide to bat identification in Great Britain and Ireland.* London. The Mammal Society & Vincent Wildlife Trust.

Opposite: *Hibernating greater horseshoe bat showing structure of the fingers and toes.*